THE BEST EVE
MONEY SAVɪɴɢ ɪɪɪ ᴜ
FOR CYCLISTS

Creative Ways to Cut Your Costs,
Conserve Your Capital and Keep Your Cash

THE BEST EVER BOOK OF
MONEY SAVING TIPS
FOR CYCLISTS

*Creative Ways to Cut Your Costs,
Conserve Your Capital and Keep Your Cash*

By Mark Geoffrey Young

Dolyttle & Seamore
New York, NY

The Best Ever Book of Money Saving Tips: Creative Ways to Cut Your Costs, Conserve Your Capital and Keep Your Cash

Dolyttle & Seamore
New York

Dolyttle & Seamore
198 Garth Road Suite 2DD
Scarsdale, NY 10583

Publisher's Cataloging-in-Publication Data

The Best Ever Guide To Demotivation: *How To Dismay, Dishearten and Disappoint Your Friends, Family and Staff*

p. cm.
ISBN-13: 9781489564269
ISBN-10: 1489564268

10 9 8 7 6 5 4 3 2 1

Mark Geoffrey Young;

For my fantastic wife Pam, who doesn't quite get
what I do, but lets me do it anyway.

FOREWARD

When it comes to money, the only people who know more about spending and saving it than Cyclists, are those people who get paid to write about it. That's right; reporters, writers and editors think they have special skills to write about every topic.

Back in the day, reporters, journalists and editors underwent years of training, explored a variety of different areas and became knowledgeable in a couple of topics. When they interviewed an expert, they were able to ask intelligent questions, build upon their knowledge, and pass this new information on to their valued readers.

Then, things changed. Al Gore invented the Internet and everybody was an instant expert. There was more information available than you could imagine. You no longer had to read about the topics in a few publications— because information (not all of it reliable) was available everywhere—and it was free.

Newspapers and magazine owners realized that since everybody was an expert, there was no need to hire talented reporters to fill up their pages because all of the information they needed could be compiled by anybody able to type www.google.com into their browser.

While this reduced the costs of publishing magazines and newspapers, everything started to look the same because all of the information came from the same place—the

Internet, instead of trusted sources. Since there was very little to distinguish one publication from the next, readers started to desert their local newspapers and speciality publications, which resulted in less original research, which led to fewer readers, which led to ... you get the idea.

Personal finance was one area that was filled with generic—and often bad—advice. Before you knew it, every publication was filled with "money saving tips" that had no relationship to the publication where they appeared. And to make it worse, some of these tips were so obvious, you knew what you were going to read, before you read it.

This book is part of the new journalism, Rather than writing original material or forcing you search the Internet—I've repackaged the best tips, the worst tips and everything in-between into this convenient book titled: The Best Ever Book of Money Saving Tips.

Some of the tips are good. Some of the tips are bad. Some of the tips are silly. Some of the tips are really silly. And, some tips are so silly, it's hard to believe that an expert was paid to write them—but since everybody is an expert—it's true. If some of the tips seem like clichés, consider clichés the new journalism.

As much as I hate clichés, you can't fight progress because a dollar is a dollar, and a penny earned is a penny saved. While money makes the world go round, it's important to save every cent. Regardless of your philosophy, there is no such thing as a free lunch.

Because money does not grow on trees, it's important to work hard to bring home the bacon. Even though Cyclists are underpaid and overworked, we know that we can't ask our filthy rich bosses for more money because we don't want to bite the hand that feeds us.

As Cyclists, we know that we must stretch our dollars, so that we'll have something left for a rainy day. If we fail, we'll be on the way to the poorhouse before we know it. Remember, there are plenty of people who will take the shirt off our backs if given half a chance, because a fool and his money are easily parted.

Even though Cyclists are not rolling in dough, we'll get cleaned out if we're not careful, and before we know it, we won't have a penny to our name. While there are more important things in life than money, and we know that money can't buy happiness, we need to be on our guard because we're not ready to cash in our chips.

To say the least, these clichés are too rich for my blood.

Mark Young
New York, New York

Dental floss is necessary but expensive. Save money by recycling it. After you're done, rinse it and hang it up to dry. Some people can get four to five uses out of each strand.

Every person will eventually get holes in their socks. When your socks need to be darned, don't waste money on an expensive darning block. Instead, use an old-fashioned round light bulb. It works just as well, and you can use the bulb for its intended purpose later.

Don't buy old wine. Every day thousands of Cyclists get sucked into the "older wine is better" trap and pay huge dollars for a single bottle of wine.

More and more Cyclists are reducing their food and catering costs by dumpster diving. Simply find a restaurant, bakery or supermarket with great reviews and hang out until they close. As soon as the coast is clear, climb into the dumpster and eat whatever takes your fancy. If you're looking for food for a party, taste everything first to make sure it meets your standards.

Search the Internet for free products. It's amazing how many companies will give Cyclists free samples of shampoo, toothpaste and other amazing products.

When you invite friends over for a barbecue, put less meat in each hamburger patty. If it's OK for large companies to reduce the size of their food packages, it's OK for Cyclists to do the same with their guests.

Save money on a gym membership by getting off the bus or train a few stops earlier. As well as getting fit, you'll save money by jumping off before the zone changes.

Laundry is an area where it's easy to waste money. An easy way to reduce costs is to dry your clothes half way and then place them on chairs, doorknobs or on counters to dry. The only reason to dry them part of the way is to prevent water damage. If you don't care about this, save even more money by not drying your clothes at all.

—·—

Exercise more. If you use your exercise bike instead of watching television, you'll reduce the amount of electricity you use by keeping the TV off. Save even more money by exercising in the dark.

—·—

Detergent companies think Cyclists are stupid and always recommend using more product than necessary. Save big bucks by reducing the recommended amount of detergent by half to two-thirds.

—·—

If you're one of those Cyclists who never gets sick, cancel your health insurance. Companies make all their money on people like you. If you do get sick, every hospital must treat you by law.

—·—

Phantom electricity costs a fortune. Reduce the amount of energy you waste by disconnecting your doorbell whenever you go out.

An easy way to reduce your food and drink bill is to water down all of your liquid foods and drinks. Your spaghetti sauce, mustard, ketchup and juices will last a lot longer if you add a little water.

———•———

Don't waste money on new clothes when you put on a few extra pounds. Instead of buying new pants, use a rubber band to expand the waist of your favorite jeans.

———•———

Cyclists know that it's expensive to replace the carpet in your home. Make your carpets last longer by placing shower caps over your shoes when you walk around the house. Not only will you prevent the carpets from getting marked, you'll also reduce the amount of cleaning supplies you need to purchase.

———

Reduce your grilling costs by buying cheaper hamburger meat. Most people put so much sauce on their burgers that they'll never know what grade of meat you bought.

———

Smart Cyclists know that detergent builds up in your dishwasher and washing machine. Cut your costs by washing without detergent every second time.

———

Many Cyclists enjoy a cup of hot tea during the day. Save money by drying out your tea bag and reusing it later. Some people have been know to get three, four or even five cups out of a single bag.

———

Spending time outdoors is a great way to save money, but all Cyclists know that it's expensive to maintain a garden. One way to reduce your gardening costs, is to use hair as a slug repellent for your plants. Ask all of your local hairdressers you can cart away the hair they sweep up from the floor. Simply sprinkle the hair around your plants and hope that the wind doesn't blow it everywhere. If you need to earn extra money, you can package the hair in small envelopes and sell it to your neighbors.

Babies are expensive because they need to be fed and clothed. Cutting the feet off baby clothes is a easy way get a few extra months of wear out of each outfit. Since babies are too young to care about their image, you won't even get any complaints.

Water is a precious resource that is often wasted. Reduce your water bill by buying a bucket and filling it with your used bath water. Use this water for your plants. Not only will you save money, you'll build up your muscles and improve your health from all this additional aerobic activity.

Save money on your wedding by shortening the planning timeline. Having a last-minute wedding greatly reduces the number of potential attendees. This cuts the amount of food you need to purchase, and generally has only a minimal effect on the number of gifts you'll receive.

—•—

Cyclists know that a lot of money is wasted in the bathroom. Put a brick in the tank above the toilet to reduce the amount of water you flush town the toilet. If you already have a water saving tank, you'll save even more.

—•—

Instead of buying costly micro beers and trendy wines, make your own at home. It's not that difficult when you have the right equipment. Don't waste money buying it new, as there are thousands of people trying to get rid of this stuff on eBay and Craig's list.

—•—

If your electricity company offers off-peak power, start your renovations after midnight when the cheaper rates kick in. This will lower your renovation costs, and when you're finished, nobody will know any better.

—•—

If you live in a warm climate, paint the roof of your car white. This cuts the inside temperature and reduces the need for air conditioning. If you live in a cool climate, paint your car roof black to reduce the need to use your car heater.

———·———

Instead of hiring professional painters to paint your house, invite all your friends over for a house-painting party. Even if you provide everybody with pizza and soda when the job is complete, the cost will still be less than having to pay professionals.

———·———

Save money shaving by using soap on your face instead of shaving cream. While this may seem like a huge sacrifice, you'll hardly notice the difference after you've been doing it for a few years.

———·———

Cyclists have always known how to reduce the amount of money they spend on consumer goods. A good way to save money on expensive binoculars, is to stand closer to the object you're trying to see.

———·———

Tanning beds are expensive. Instead of wasting your time and money trying to look good, simply pop your used tea bags in the bath and soak until your skin turns the color you desire.

If you don't have much trash, cancel your service and put everything in your neighbor's garbage can. Do this late at night, so nobody will notice. Take care to remove your address from the old mail—just in case.

Instead of buying a new grill at the beginning of spring so you can enjoy barbecuing with your friends, wait until the fall when the stores mark down their prices. While you may miss one summer of fun, the savings will pay off if you're planning to live for a long time.

Weddings are a huge expense for Cyclists. Instead of wasting money on expensive attire that costs a fortune, add an unusual twist on your big day by wearing the clothes you both had on the day you met. This will attract additional attention if you met bike riding, at a swimming pool or during a loved one's funeral.

Add a fireplace to your home. This will pay off over time because a continually burning wood fire will keep the temperature in your home constant, reducing the need for expensive, gas, electric or oil heat.

Instead of wasting money on gifts for your family and friends, give them something personal such as baby-sitting. Your grandchildren or children will enjoy at trip to the playground with you almost as much as an expensive electronic gadget. Not only will you save money, you'll spend time bonding. Studies show that teenagers with a happy family life are less likely to do drugs or alcohol.

Even though Cyclists work harder than most other people, your friends know that you're entitled to a break. Exploit this by telling everybody that you'll be out of town for the holidays.

Not only will you earn extra interest on your savings, you'll get to shop in January when everything is on sale.

———•———

Cyclists know that foods can be used for a variety of different purposes. After you've eaten an avocado, rub the inside of the skin against your face, as it makes a great face pack. After your skin is soft, use the skin to buff your shoes.

———•———

Cyclists have been reducing the costs of bringing up children for years by sending them off to play at a friend's home after school and on weekends. Even if your kids don't get a dinner invitation, they'll always get a snack.

———•———

Cyclists are always being invited to different celebrations: birthdays; weddings; anniversaries; etc. Reduce your outlays by reusing the cards people have given you. Simply place the used greeting card on a south-facing window with the sender's writing facing outward. The sun will eventually bleach the writing white: eliminating the need to purchase a new card. WARNING: To avoid offending your friends, take care not to send it back to the person who originally sent to you because they'll think that you're really cheap.

———•———

Carry less cash in your wallet or pocket book. That way, if you're robbed, the mugger will get less of your hard-earned money.

Rinse out your used condoms, turn them inside out and hang them up to dry after you've done. Double your savings, and reduce the risk of offending your next partner, by keeping the lights off at all times.

———

Save the water you used to boil the pasta for soup. Since soup is mostly water, all you have to do is throw in a few vegetables and some meat into the pot and your next meal is ready.

———

Make your toilet paper last longer by squashing the entire roll into an oval shape. While it's harder to unroll each sheet, the inconvenience is well worth the effort since everybody will use less and each roll will last longer.

No matter what sort of heat you use at home: oil; gas; or electric, it's expensive. An easy way to reduce your heating bills is to wear extra clothes around your house and wrap yourself in blankets when it gets really cold.

Regardless of how much money you spend on your kids, they always want more. Instead of wasting money on expensive electronic music players, teach them to hum. If they don't like the music that's playing, they can always think of a different tune and hum that.

Cyclists hate waste. Instead of wasting the water you used to bathe in, grab a bucket and use it to flush your toilet.

Showers are a complete waste of money. Reduce the amount of money you waste by getting your body wet and turning off the water. Then, soap your body, shampoo your hair and turn the water back on. You should be able to have a three-minute shower in under a minute. Cyclists know that they can save even more money by using cold water.

———•———

If you use a fireplace or woodstove to heat your home, wait until spring to stock up on firewood. It's much cheaper than buying it during winter, and you can always improvise to get through the long, cold months.

———•———

Cyclists love to travel for a bargain. Save money on your wedding by holding it in a small town that's miles away from those expensive city venues. Since these venues are generally underused, they'll quote you a great price to host your event.

———•———

Teach your children the value of a dollar by walking them to school. Not only will your children be healthier, they'll build up immunity to a variety of diseases by going out in the rain, sun and snow. While your children may not appreciate your efforts now, they'll thank you for your thoughtfulness later in life.

———•———

Don't waste money on expensive haircuts. Instead, visit

your local hairdressing school. While the cut may be less than perfect, you're doing a good deed by giving a future professional the confidence he or she needs to start their career off on a positive note.

———

Many towns will give you a free tree. Take your free tree and place it in front of a window that gets a lot of sun. This will reduce the need to run your air conditioning.

———

Become a vegan. Meat and dairy products are expensive. By eliminating them from your diet and replacing them with cheaper fruits and vegetables, you save money, and become healthier.

———

Steam open all you mail instead of tearing it apart so you can reuse your used envelopes when you need to mail something out. Sticky labels are a lot cheaper than envelopes and most people will appreciate the effort you're making to protect the environment.

———

Throw out your clock radio and buy a wind up clock to cut your energy costs. While you do have to remember to wind it every night, Cyclists know that every penny saved is two pennies earned—because you don't have to pay taxes on the money you save.

———•———

Every Cyclist loves flowers, but they're expensive. Cut your costs and give your partner the love he or she needs by stopping off at the cemetery on your way home from work.

———•———

When renovating a home, Cyclists know that they can save money by putting in fewer outlets and light fixtures. Just remember that everything you buy costs money, and the less you buy, the less you spend.

———•———

Whenever you eat at a fast food restaurant, save the cup so you won't have to order a drink next time you stop in for a quick meal.

———•———

Alcohol is an expensive part of every wedding. Save money by holding a "prohibition" themed event to reduce your costs. Everybody will talk about your event for years to come.

———•———

Everybody believes that the light on your refrigerator turns

When painting your house, choose the same color for every room. This will reduce the number of half-empty cans of paint you have laying around when you've finished the job.

off when you close the door. But does it really? Eliminate all doubts by unscrewing the bulb and reusing it in a part of your house where it can make a difference.

— · —

Cut your laundry bills in half by turning your underwear inside out so you can wear it twice before it needs to be washed. Unless you're a really smelly Cyclist, nobody will notice the difference.

— · —

Get a part time job in a restaurant. Most places will give you a free meal after your complete your shift—and some restaurants will even let you take your customers' leftover food home. You'll also earn a few extra dollars that will come in handy on a rainy day.

———

Reduce the costs of running your home by disconnecting the gas, electricity and water. Cyclists know that all of these luxuries cost money. Eliminating them is the first step on the road to prosperity.

———

Make your pets earn their keep. If you have two cats, train one to sit on your lap and the other to sit on your neck to reduce your heating bills.

———

Go to the bathroom before you leave work and tell your children to do the same before they leave school. Nobody knows for sure how much you'll save, but you can bet it's more than you think when you factor in the costs of water, electricity and toilet paper.

———

Gas is expensive. Reduce the amount of fuel you use by

turning off your car engine whenever you get stuck in traffic or at a red light.

———•———

Many Cyclists waste money at the supermarket. Before you check out, remove everything from your shopping cart, and only put the items that you actually need back in. You'll find 20 to 30 percent of the stuff you put in the cart is unnecessary.

———•———

Cancel all your mail order catalogs. Reducing the temptation to buy is an easy way to reduce your spending. Simply send a letter to the merchant whose catalog you received and ask them to take you off their list. After all, they only want to mail their junk mail to people who are actually going to buy.

———•———

Turn off your engine and place your car in neutral whenever you're going downhill to reduce your gas bill.

———•———

Drink more water. By sipping on a glass of water instead of eating something when you're hungry, you can reduce your yearly food bill by thousands of dollars. Maximize the savings by filling up a container with water from work.

Instead of hiring a professional photographer for your wedding, hire a student. With digital cameras there's very little that can go wrong. Just because your special day is a once-in-a-lifetime event, doesn't mean you have to let every professional take advantage of you.

Give your children wind-up flashlights to move around the house. By only allowing one light to be used in your house at a time, your savings will grow over time.

Save money on children's birthday parties by holding them in the afternoon instead of at lunch—or dinner-time. Instead of having to provide pizza and other snacks, you'll only need to offer the little ones cake and ice cream.

———•———

Invest in a rainwater tank for your home and put buckets under all your gutters. Saving all this water allows Cyclists to reduce their water bills to almost nothing. If the water is too dirty to drink, you can still use it to flush your toilets, water your garden and wash your car.

———•———

Instead of wasting money on toilet paper, use your junk mail. It's sent to your home almost every day, and it's always in plentiful supply. Just be careful to remove any staples or fake plastic credit cards before you use it.

———•———

Whenever you get into a car or other vehicle, adjust your sunglasses before you start the engine to reduce the amount of money you spend on gas. With the rising cost of gas, every little bit helps.

———•———

Cyclists can reduce their motoring costs by eliminating excess weight from their vehicles. Remove the back seat, spare tire, floor mats and mirrors from your car or van.

An easy way to reduce your motoring expenses is to avoid repairing your car when it breaks down. Smart Cyclists know that if your car is immobile, it doesn't need gas. Not having to put gas in your car reduces your costs and increases the amount of money in your bank account.

Dairy products are expensive. Reduce the cost of every cup of tea or coffee by drinking it black. Not having to add an extra ingredient into your cup saves time—as well as money.

Don't waste your money going to the movies. Instead, get a friend to tell you what happened.

An easy area to save money on at a wedding is on the flowers. Many Cyclists are cutting their costs by designing the centerpieces themselves or asking a friend to take on this commitment as a favor. While this is a time-consuming process—and the results may not be the same as hiring a professional—you don't want to waste money on your special day.

Washing dishes is expensive because you have to pay for both water and dish detergent. Save money washing up by placing cling wrap over your dishes before you put any food on them.

————•—•———

Carpooling is often overlooked when it comes to saving money. Even if your schedule doesn't quite match up with your co-workers, nothing feels as good as saving money—even if it's totally inconvenient for you and your workers.

————•—•———

An easy way to reduce your motoring costs in the city is to turn off the air conditioning in your vehicle on very hot days. While air conditioning may keep your kids calm, reduce road rage and keep you sane, it costs money. Eliminating this unnecessary luxury can increase your gas mileage by 10 to 20 percent.

————•—•———

When your towels wear out, cut them down in size, hem them and use them as washcloths. Multi-colored bathrooms are the new "in" thing.

————•—•———

Save money on renovations by reusing the old cabinets, toilets, floorboards, etc. To reduce your renovation costs, even more, skip the entire job and leave things the way they are now. If you're planning to sell your home in a couple of years, the new owners will probably want to do things their own way, so you'll never recover your investment.

———•———

When traveling, reduce your accommodation costs by taking a redeye flight or overnight train. Most clients will overlook your mistakes and cut you a break if they know you're exhausted.

———•———

An easy way to reduce your food costs is to buy the food that's on sale at the supermarket. Instead of buying meals that you like, buy what's cheap and watch your savings grow.

———•———

Instead of renting out an amusement park or expensive venue for your child's birthday party, hold it in your home. While you may get a few groans, giving your children everything they want is not they way to create balanced adults.

———•———

Smart Cyclists know that their bank offers a variety of services. Many of them even provide coffee and lollypops for

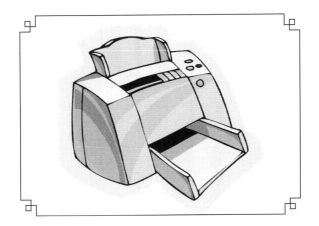

Save money on printing by keeping the paper tray empty in your computer printer. If every time you want to print a document you have to put paper in the paper tray, you'll print fewer documents.

free. Choose a financial institution that's close to work and stock up on your way to or from work.

———•———

Save money by turning off your TV. Since a television needs electricity to work, keeping the switch in the "off" position will considerably reduce your costs over time.

———•———

Instead of buying expensive mailing tubes, use the tubes that held your paper towels. While they may be a bit smaller than commercial tubes, you can always bend your artwork to make it fit.

———•———

Never buy umbrellas. Every Cyclist knows the easy way to stay dry in a rainstorm is to find old umbrellas in the trash and turn them into stylish ponchos. Once you get the hang of it, you could even turn this little activity into a profitable business.

———•———

Cyclists spend a lot of money in the bathroom. One way to reduce your costs is to reduce the number of times you flush your toilet. For most families, once a day is fine, but if you only have a few people in your home, you could probably get away with a couple of times a week.

———•———

Airports and train stations make great hotels. Instead of booking an expensive hotel, simply stretch out over the airport furniture and make yourself at home. Not only do airports and train stations have an unlimited number of bathrooms, they have a huge variety of eating establishments.

———•———

An easy way to save money is to buy everything you need at stores that charge less than expensive stores.

———•———

Don't buy bags for dog poop. Instead, use the bag your newspaper came in, or stock up on the free plastic bags that most supermarkets give away.

———•———

Just because most Cyclists like wine, doesn't mean you have to waste your money on a wine refrigerator. Your basement is the ideal place to store your liquid nourishment.

———•———

Don't waste your money on an expensive piggy bank to store all your spare change. Instead, use an old coffee can and take it to the bank when it fills up.

———•———

Reduce your outlay on formal clothes, handbags and jewelry by renting them online. Because you don't actually own the

Find God. Religious people spend more time praying and looking upward for salvation instead of wasting time at the mall looking for material possessions to satisfy their worldly desires.

stuff, you can move into a smaller house and reduce your living costs even more.

———•———

Since Cyclists are more productive than every other worker, you don't need to spend as much time at the office as everybody else. Reduce your transport costs by coming in late and leaving early. Sitting in traffic is very expensive.

———•———

When it comes to cleaning supplies, never buy the well-known brands. Instead buy generics or visit your local dollar store: Winex is the almost the same as Windex and Agax is as close as you can get to Ajax. If you don't believe me, look at how similar the packaging is. The main reason these brands are cheaper is because they don't waste their money on advertising.

———•———

If you've ever tried to buy a doorstop, you know how expensive they are. Save your money by finding large rocks and covering them in tinfoil. Everybody will be impressed by your creativity.

———•———

Eliminate babysitting costs and earn additional cash by renting out your kids to couples who are thinking about starting a family. They get to see what children are like and you provide valuable community service to those people who aren't sure about their future responsibilities.

———•———

Cyclists know that food is food. Instead of wasting money on expensive organic produce, buy the stuff that's sprayed with pesticides. It's cheaper, and generally looks better than the organic fruits and vegetables because the bugs haven't been able to attack it.

———•———

Back massagers are not only expensive to purchase, they're expensive to run. Instead of wasting your hard earned cash on this useless appliance, grab an old stocking and fill it with tennis balls. Your back will never notice the difference.

———·———

Limit the number of children your child can have at their birthday party, Instead of inviting the entire class, invite only five or ten kids. While they many moan and groan, it's important for their classmates to learn about rejection at an early age.

———·———

Even though many newspapers are available free online, some people do like the dead-tree edition. Save your money on newspapers by going down to your train or bus station and taking them out of the recycling bin.

———·———

Save all of your change and watch it add up. Instead of giving it to the useless bum on the corner, put it in a jar in your kitchen. You'll be surprised how fast it adds up.

———·———

If you own a small business, you can reduce your wedding expenses by sponsoring your own wedding and including it in your advertising budget. If done properly, you may even be able to generate extra business for your company.

—•—

Since Cyclists often have to get to the airport for their next vacation, how you get there can make or break your trip. Instead of taking an expensive limo, you can usually get there with a combination of trains, buses and taxis. While it may take longer, you and your children will have extra money to spend when you get to your destination.

—•—

Most fast food outlets offer great deals on breakfast. Save money by stopping off on your way to work and storing the meal in your desk draw until lunchtime. Sandwiches will last for quite a while before they actually go bad.

—•—

Get rid of your pets. Those cute fuzzy animals are costing you a fortune. An easy way to dramatically improve your financial position is to sell your pets.

—•—

Don't waste money on office supplies. Whenever you need a pen, visit your local bank. More and more financial institutions are giving away FREE pens and other samples such as coffee than ever before.

———•———

Every movie theater and club has a back door or fire escape. Save the admission fee by walking through this door backwards. If you get caught, at least you'll be facing the right way when you have to run.

———•———

Supermarkets offer a variety of free samples. Stop by to check out what they're offering whenever you're hungry.

———•———

Houses, apartments and mobile homes are all overrated. Reduce your housing costs by living in your car. Not only will you save on rent, you'll also eliminate a variety of ancillary costs such as electricity, water and heat.

———•———

If your child gets too many presents at their birthday, return the extras or save them as gifts for the next party your child has to attend. Just make sure you don't re-gift the present to the same person who gave it to you.

Replace your electric shaver with a single blade hand razor. You can you pick up one cheaply at a tag sale. Since blades are cheap, and you don't use electricity, you'll save a fortune.

Instead of renting a clown or performer for your child's birthday party, find a cheap costume online and dress up as that character. If you're too busy to do this, get a friend or relative to do the honors.

Complaining is an easy way for Cyclists to get things for free. Regardless of whether you're eating at a restaurant, buying a service, or getting surgery: complaining about everything will generally get you something for free—or at least reduce the cost of whatever you're buying.

—·—

An easy way to reduce your electricity costs is to put your freezer on a timer. By setting the timer to turn on and off every 12 hours, you'll cut the cost of running this appliance in half. Most of the items in the freezer won't have a problem with this—as long as you don't ever open the door.

—·—

An easy way to reduce your gas costs is to drive behind large trucks and coast down the hills. Drafting behind trucks in neutral cuts wind resistance and reduces your fuel costs. Just remember to turn your engine back on when you hit a flat piece of road, because your car is not a perpetual motion machine.

—·—

Pets can save you lots of money. Instead of buying expensive blankets or paying for heat, adopt a large dog from the pound. Using your new best friend as a blanket will reduce your heating costs considerably.

—·—

Buy all your cans of soda at the supermarket and store them in your car. Whenever you purchase a meal at the drive-through, ask for a cup of ice, and you'll never have to pay for a cold drink again.

—•—

Recycling is a smart way to save money. Cyclists all over the world are coming up with new and innovate ways to reduce their costs. Instead of buying handkerchiefs, cut an old T-shirt or tablecloth to the correct size and place this in your pocket.

—•—

Sandwich bags are expensive. Don't buy them. Instead, save the liners from cereal boxes and use them instead. These bags are so large so you can place several sandwiches in them at a time, making it possible for all your children to bring their lunch to school in one convenient package.

—•—

Shop at libraries, bus terminals, churches and other institutions that have lost and found boxes. It's possible to get almost everything you need from a simple black umbrella to a complete set of dentures at these venues.

—•—

Buy a sheep to reduce your lawn-mowing bill. Not only will the sheep keep your grass short, it will provide you with free fertilizer and wool to make your own clothes. You also have a ready food source in case of famine.

More and more Cyclists have decided that eating is overrated. Instead of wasting time and energy eating three meals every day, cut your costs by only preparing only one meal per day. Not only will you save money on food, you'll also reduce your water, electricity and gas costs as you'll be spending less time in the kitchen.

Cities and towns make a lot of money by gouging ordinary motorists big bucks to park their cars. Show how smart

Cyclists are by driving your car around and around until you find a meter with time on it.

— • —

If you have more than one bedroom in your house, save money by putting your children in one room, and renting out the other bedrooms to needy strangers. Not only will you generate much needed rent money, you'll also pick up a free baby sitter if you're clever enough to put this stipulation in the lease.

— • —

If your wedding budget is very tight, consider printing your own wedding invites on your personal computer. It won't take long—and even if they're not 100 percent right, most people will be so happy to be on your invitation list that they won't have the nerve to say anything.

— • —

If you're planning a vacation of a lifetime, reduce your costs by picking a destination close to home. Choosing an exotic location can require visas, passports and expensive airfares. Staying close to home can reduce your costs by 90 percent or more. If your friends ask where you went, simply print out some photographs from the Web.

— • —

An easy way to cut your living costs to virtually nothing is to find a rich sugar daddy or sugar mommy who is willing to pay for everything you need, want and desire.

—·—

Hot weather can get the best of every Cyclist. Instead of wasting money on expensive air conditioning, head on over to the library and read all their books and magazines for free. Maximize your savings by taking the entire family along. That way you know exactly where everybody is—and you know that nobody is spending any money.

—·—

Cyclists are great partiers. Take advantage of your skills by gate crashing weddings, parties, funerals and other celebrations. Not only will you get to meet new people, you'll save a fortune on food and drink. Just remember to dress the part, or you may find yourself out the door before you can find out what your next event is.

—·—

If you live in an apartment or a house that's close to your neighbors, get free Internet by cracking your neighbor's WI-FI password.

—·—

Give up smoking and eliminate alcohol, beer, soda, drugs, cakes, candy and other unnecessary items from your diet. While your life may be less enjoyable, you'll save money, be healthier and live longer.

Many colleges welcome Cyclists and run courses that show you how to do things yourself. A simple car mechanic course can save you thousands of dollars over a lifetime—and can even lead to additional income if you're willing to share your new-found skills with your friends and neighbors.

—•—

Don't waste water washing your car. Simply wait until it rains and rush out with your detergent and rags. Before you know it, you'll have a clean car for a fraction of the normal price.

Pee in the shower or tub. Not only will you save money on water, you'll save time and be able to get a lot more things done in your day.

———•———

Replace your dishes with smaller plates. Putting less food on your plate means you'll eat less—because nobody wants to seem like a pig and ask for more. This is especially effective if you host a lot of dinner parties.

———•———

Remove all of the extra bath towels from your bathroom. If you only hang up a couple of towels for your entire family to use, you'll extend the life of your washing machine by using it less, and cut your detergent, water and electric bills.

———•———

To make extra money, ask your payroll office to take less tax out of your pay each week. Place this money in an interest-bearing bank account and watch your money grow. If you end up owning money at the end of the year, you can always give it back to the taxman when you file your taxes.

———•———

Every month have a no-spend weekend, and every quarter have a no-spend week. By forcing yourself to not spend any of your hard-earned cash, you get to save your money for a rainy day when you really need it.

———•———

Don't claim on your car insurance. Even though you pay for insurance in case of an accident, claiming on your policy almost always forces up your rates. Not claiming on your insurance is an easy way to ensure that you always pay the lowest possible rate.

———•———

Eat your food cold. Ovens, toasters, grills and microwaves all cost money to run. By eliminating the need to heat up your food, you can save a considerable amount of money.

———•———

Never, ever throw out your expired food. Even though your cheese may be moldy, and your grapes mushy, keeping your fridge full reduces your electric bill and extends the life of your refrigerator. The emptier your refrigerator is, the harder it has to work to keep everything cold.

———•———

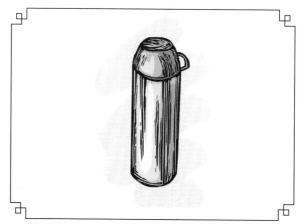

Reduce your electricity and water bill by filling your thermos with hot water before you leave work. That way you can make yourself a cup of tea or coffee at home for virtually nothing.

After you've finished using a paper towel, wash it out and hang it up to dry. Careful Cyclists are able to get two to three uses out of every paper towel.

———•———

Stock up on chicken, turkey and other meats when they're on sale. When you get home, grind up all your meats and throw them in the freezer for a few months. While your meats may taste a little funny due to freezer-burn, it's unlikely that you'll get sick. Experts say that most meat can be safely frozen for six months or so.

No matter how miserable your life is, stay married. Even poor Cyclists know that getting divorced is expensive, time consuming and a waste of money.

Reuse your vacuum bags. Instead of throwing them out when they're full, simply shake out the insides into a large garbage can and vacuum up the mess. Since these bags are so strong, you should be able to get many uses out of each one.

Don't buy new picture frames. If you're looking for a cheap frame, visit as many flea markets and garage sales as possible. Don't be put off by the old print, photograph or painting in the frame. By concentrating only on the frame, you can get a great bargain. Sometimes the clearance sections of department stores have even better deals than tag sales. And remember, you can always paint or re-stain the frame if the color isn't to your liking.

An easy way to reduce the cost of bath time for your children is to purchase a single bottle of the shampoo that they like and refill it with the cheap stuff you get at the dollar store. Most children can't tell the difference, and if they can, just tell them the manufacturer must have changed the formulation. Most of the time, kids don't really care what's in the bottle, they just want to use the trendy stuff that their friends use.

———•———

Wash your own car. Constantly paying someone to do this simple task is expensive and unnecessary. If you live in an apartment complex, invest in a hose and borrow some water from your neighbors late at night when they're sleeping.

———•———

Area rugs cost a fortune. One easy way that smart Cyclists can reduce their home renovation costs, is to drive around and look at the houses being renovated. When you find some discarded carpet, grab it. Look at it closely and work out which parts of the carpet have not been walked on (under the bed, couch and dresser), and cut an area rug out of this space. If you want the rug to last, pick up some binding and glue at your local carpet store to bind the edges.

———•———

Stop throwing away paper napkins. Instead, invest in some cheap cloth ones. While you may not notice the savings immediately, they will add up over time.

Instead of taking you car to a mechanic when it needs work, visit your local vocational school. Since the students are being trained, most schools will do the work for free—although you may have to pay for parts. Today's cars are easier to work on than those of yesteryear—an easy-to-use computer diagnostic tool quickly works out what needs to be done. As a result, there's very little that the kids can get wrong.

Since Cyclists are simple people, it easy to stay entertained. Instead of visiting your local museums, zoos, botanic gardens and other area attractions when it's convenient, call them up and ask when they have free days. Mark these on you calendar. By planning these trips well in advance, you get to enjoy the attraction twice: once when you think about them; and once when you actually go.

Cyclists know that medical costs are constantly rising. One way to reduce your eyeglass costs is to buy your frames at a flea market, garage sale, or other venue. While these glasses may be a little bent, chipped or used, they're perfectly serviceable. Take them to your local eye doctor and ask him or her to cut lenses to fit these frames.

Here's a tip that smart Cyclists used during the depression. Instead of buying your kids shoes that fit, purchase a pair that's two or three sizes too big, so their feet can grow into them. While you wait, stuff the extra space with newspaper so their feet don't slide all over the place.

———•———

Always buy the same brand and color of socks because socks don't wear out evenly. When you get a hole in one sock, simply combine the other sock with a friend. Save the worn socks so you can use them when you run out of laundry.

———•———

Forget about convenience. Instead of storing your credit card number with online retailers, enter it every time. This extra effort will greatly reduce the amount of stuff you by online. Also, you'll spend so much time entering and reentering wrong numbers, you won't have time to shop.

———•———

Instead of buying toilet paper, invest in a hand-held bidet sprayer. Over a period of time, you'll recoup your investment many times over.

———•———

Eat a huge meal before you go shopping. Studies have

After you've used a tissue, iron it and put back in the box for later. You'll be surprised at how few people know about this money saving tip.

shown that people with full stomachs buy less at the supermarket because their minds are elsewhere. Remember, if you forget something, you can always go back the next day or pick it up at your local convenience store.

———•———

Even though Cyclists are very efficient people, they often over-estimate their capabilities and try to do too many things. Reducing the number of items on your to-do list saves you money because you can drive slower to each destination. Rushing from place to place not only uses more gas, it often results in speeding tickets that cost money and force your insurance rates up.

———·———

Every Cyclist knows that the perfect time to buy calendars and day planners is in January when they're on sale. Unfortunately you may need to start planning events in November and December when they're expensive. However, a little bit of planning can result in big savings.

Your 2013 calendar can be used in 2019, 2030, 2041
Your 2014 calendar can be used in 2025, 2031, 2042
Your 2015 calendar can be used in 2026, 2037, 2043
Your 2016 calendar can be used in 2044, 2072, 2112
Your 2017 calendar can be used in 2017, 2023, 2034
Your 2018 calendar can be used in 2029, 2035, 2045
Your 2019 calendar can be used in 2030, 2041, 2047
Your 2020 calendar can be used in 2048, 2076, 2116

Just remember that while the days of the week will line up perfectly, the holidays won't. Get around this by marking the new holidays on the calendar with a black, felt tip pen.

———·———

While we're on the topic of old calendars, you can also save substantial amounts of money by purchasing old calendars from tag sales, flea markets and other sources that sell old junk.

In 2014, you can reuse calendars from 2003, 1997, 1986,

1975, 1969, 1958, 1947, 1941, 1930, and 1919.

In 2015, you can reuse calendars from 2009, 1998, 1987, 1981, 1970, 1959, 1953, 1942, 1931, and 1925.

In 2016, you can reuse calendars from 1988, 1960, and 1932.

In 2017, you can reuse calendars from 2006, 1995, 1989, 1978, 1967, 1961, 1950, 1939, 1933, and 1922.

In 2018, you can reuse calendars from 2007, 2001, 1990, 1979, 1973, 1962, 1951, 1945, 1934, and 1923.

In 2019, you can reuse calendars from 2013, 2002, 1991, 1985, 1974, 1963, 1957, 1946, 1935, and 1929.

In 2020, you can reuse calendars from 1992, 1964, and 1936.

Just remember that while the days of the week will line up perfectly, the holidays won't. Get around this by marking the new holidays on the calendar with a black, felt tip pen.

———•———

Most Cyclists fail to realize that the toothpaste tube isn't really empty when you can't squeeze any more product out of it. Instead of throwing the "empty" tube in recycling, cut it down the middle with an art knife. You can generally get an extra two or three brushings out of each tube.

Reduce your entertainment costs by freezing a tube of toothpaste and cutting it into thin slices. These slices make excellent after-dinner mints and can cost a fraction of what mints cost.

———•———

Almost every Cyclist screws up occasionally and pays their credit card, mortgage or other bill late. Instead of paying the late charges, call up your credit card company and spin them a line about how you're recovering from open-heart surgery or tell them that you just managed to smuggle your great-grandmother out of war-torn Bermuda or some other exotic country.

———•———

At the end of each day, put all of your $10 bills in a jar and save it for a rainy day. You'll be surprised how quickly this money adds up. At the end of the year, you should have more than $3,000 in the jar. Most people won't notice the difference. And, if you do, you can always go to an ATM for more money. Just make sure to pick a fee-free ATM.

Cut the cost of eating out in restaurants in half by asking for a doggie bag before your food arrives. When the meal is placed before you, cut it in half and place the part you're not going to eat in the container. This not only reduces the temptation to overeat, it saves you from having to buy dinner tomorrow.

Buy a tent for your vacations. Instead of paying for an expensive hotel room, you can rent a camping site—or simply set up next to the road. Cyclists have found this a great way to vacation without breaking the bank.

Make your curtains last longer by painting all of the windows in your house or apartment black. This greatly reduces the amount of sunshine that enters your home. As a result, your curtains will last for years longer than they otherwise would.

Hair grows about half an inch a month. An easy way to save money is to get your hair cut less often. Instead of visiting the hairdresser every two months and getting one inch cut off, visit him or her every four months and get two inches cut off. You'll not only cut the cost of haircuts in half, you'll save even more money by only driving to the salon half as often. If your hair really starts to annoy you between haircuts, ask a friend who is good with scissors to cut off the pieces that are bothering you.

Where you live greatly affects how much money you spend. Smart Cyclists know that an easy way to reduce your costs is to move to a cheaper city or country. While it may be inconvenient to have to learn a second language later in life, the cost savings can result in some pretty big payoffs.

Food is always a major cost in any family. An easy way to reduce your food costs is to make everything from scratch. Instead of buying pre-made pizza dough, canned sauce and shredded cheese, buy raw materials. While it will take longer to mill your own flour, stew the tomatoes and shred the cheese, the savings will add up.

Reduce your electricity bills by unplugging all your appliances before you go to sleep at night, and again when you go out during the day. Many appliances such as TVs, DVRs, computers, etc., continue to draw power even when they're turned off. Putting everything on power strips makes the necessary task so much easier.

———•———

Water is not only a scarce resource, it's also very expensive. Instead of throwing out the water you used to cook dinner, tip it into a bucket. When it's cooled, take the "waste water" outside and use it to water your plants.

———•———

Whenever you leave your home, carry a notebook with you and write down the prices of everything you buy at every store. When you're in another area, visit the local supermarkets and variety stores to compare prices. If their prices are lower, pick up the items you need and add these prices to your notebook. If you have a smart phone, set up a spreadsheet in one of those easy-to-use apps to reduce the effort it takes to search.

———•———

Old products often work just as well as the new ones. Years ago, Cyclists used baking soda to clean their teeth. Truth is, this method works just as well today as it did in the past. While the taste may take some getting used to, this concoction is much cheaper than commercial toothpaste.

———•———

When driving, restrict the amount of time you leave your signal on when you make a turn. By only allowing your lights to blink one or two times, you can extend the life of each bulb considerably.

———•———

Instead of buying expensive kitty litter for your cats, teach them how to use the toilet. Not only will you reduce your costs here, you'll spend less on room deodorizer.

———•———

Many Cyclists have reduced their food costs by investing in businesses that sell food. If you eat a lot of ice cream, chicken, hamburgers, etc., consider buying a business that sells this type of food so you can purchase everything you need wholesale.

———•———

Every time you get a traffic or parking ticket go to court to contest it. If you can come up with a convincing story, the judge will generally cut the fine and eliminate or reduce the number of points on your license. You'll save money and cut

Reduce your transport costs by not buying a ticket and spending the entire train trip in the bathroom. After all, it is possible that you do have a really weak bladder.

your insurance premiums. Just tell your boss you were sick so you don't lose a day's pay.

—·—

Set the amount you are prepared to pay for clothing and stick to it. If you decide that no item of clothing can cost more than $20, don't spend more than $20 regardless of how nice it is—or how much it originally cost. Going up to $25, costs you $5 more than you budgeted. Once you start making exceptions, there's no stopping.

———•———

Most Cyclists find it easy to overeat. An easy way to reduce the amount of food you consume is to fast one day per week. By fasting on a day that you normally eat out, you can easily cut your food costs by 15 to 20 percent.

———•———

Save all your soap slivers until you have a reasonable quantity and smash them together in a small mold. With practice, you should be able to cut your soap bill by between 10 and 20 percent.

———•———

Home renovation costs are out of control and paint now costs a small fortune. By visiting tag sales in your area, you can often pick up paint remnants for a fraction of the new cost. In many cases, you can even get attractive colors that are no longer produced.

———•———

While most licensed trades people will proudly talk about their education, training and skills, many electrical, plumbing and other repairs are not as difficult as they seem. If the job is too hard for you to undertake, consider hiring one of the many unlicensed people who charge a fraction of what professionals cost. If they get it wrong, you can always hire someone with a license later.

————•————

Instead of taking your kids to an expensive private swimming pool, arrange an outing to your local town lake or beach. Most towns offer residents a discount, and these natural attractions are generally cheaper than pools.

————•————

Cyclists all over the world are reducing their electricity bills by 50 percent by removing half of the light bulbs in their homes. As well as cutting your power bill, you also reduce your bulb bill because you only have to replace half of the bulbs.

————•————

When it comes to saving money on cars, Cyclists are experts. One easy way to reduce the cost of gas is to buy a smaller car. While it may be uncomfortable to squeeze a large family into a small car, you need to decide which is more important: comfort or cost.

————•————

Save money on celebrations such as weddings and other important events by holding them on a weeknight. Not only will most places give you a great price, you'll also reduce the headcount because many of your out-of-town friends and relatives won't be able to attend.

Everybody deserves a vacation. If you're traveling and haven't booked a room for the night, negotiate when you check in. If the hotel wants too much money, go down the road. The worst thing that can happen is that you spend the night in your car—and that's not so bad because it's free.

Never buy anything new. Craig's list and eBay are filled with people selling everything you need at drastically reduced prices. While you may not be able to get the correct size, color or brand, when it comes to saving money, near enough is always good enough.

———•———

Cyclists should never have to pay bank fees. If your financial institution charges a fee, talk to the manager. If he or she refuses to remove it, withdraw all your money in cash immediately. There are hundreds of financial institutions that will happily pay for your business.

———•———

Most people put only the recommended amount of clothing in the washing machine and drier. Smart Cyclists know that you can cram a lot more stuff in than the manufacturer recommends. Doing this, cuts the number of loads you need to do, reduces the amount of laundry detergent you use, and saves electricity.

———•———

Get your gardener to cut the grass shorter than he or she usually does. This increases the time needed between cuts and dramatically reduces the amount of money you spend on your garden.

———•———

Reduce the amount of furniture you need to buy by making sure it can be used in multiple rooms. Instead of buying separate pillows for your bedroom, simply place a cover over your couch cushions and use them on your bed.

———•——

Save your soap slivers and put them into the mesh bag that your onions come in. Tie this bag together tightly and use it to wash yourself—like you would a washcloth. This eliminates waste and reduces your soap bill.

———•——

When your car tires wear out, replace them with used tires that still have life in them. This should help your cash flow—even if you do need to replace your tires more often than you previously did.

———•——

Every household wastes a lot of money in the kitchen. One way to cut the amount of money that goes down the drain is to put what's left of the cooking oil back in the bottle when you're cleaning up.

———•——

Increase your income by always looking at the road and sidewalk when you walk. It's amazing how many people drop coins and even dollar bills because they're not paying attention to what they're doing.

———•———

Cyclists are very social people. One way to save money is to go to supermarket with a friend. This allows you to pick up items you don't use often and share them with your friend. To avoid arguments, decide who gets to keep the original ketchup container and who has to supply their own before you purchase each item.

———•———

Save money on commuting by putting only half the amount of gas in your car that you usually do. If you see your tank is nearly empty, you'll make fewer trips because you won't want to put gas in your car if you don't use it that often.

———•———

Instead of buying expensive garbage bags when you're at the supermarket, use the free shopping bags that most supermarkets give away when you shop. Feel free to take a few extra, as the supermarket pays virtually nothing for each one. If your supermarket charges for bags, shop elsewhere to save money.

———•———

When you eat fruit with seeds: watermelon; apples; oranges; etc., dry out the seeds and plant them in the spring. In a few years, you'll have a beautiful garden filled with home-grown fruit that will provide you with a retirement income as well as saving you money.

———•———

Cyclists know that all fertilizer is the same. Instead of buying expensive fertilizers use your fruit, vegetable and other household waste to keep your garden green.

———•———

Unless you have a serious illness, don't waste your time going to the doctor. There are thousands of Internet sites that allow you to self-diagnose your illness at home.

———•———

Plan you home renovations carefully. If you wait until your neighbors go on vacation, you can plug an extension cord into one of their external outlets and run all of your power tools from this cord.

———•———

Cyclists who live in apartment complexes can save money by exchanging their burned out light bulbs with those in the

Reduce the amount of money you spend by freezing your credit cards in an ice cream container filled with water. Having to unfreeze your credit cards every time you need them will greatly reduce your spending.

hallways. It's not really stealing—because you already pay hefty maintenance fees.

———•———

When you're traveling in foreign countries, buy your food from the street, instead of from the fancy, overpriced restaurants that cater to tourists. You'll save money and get to experience the city like a local.

———•———

Cyclists have realized that an easy way to cut their vacation costs is to sit through a time-share presentation. In return for two or three hours of your time, many timeshare resorts will give you free accommodation or discounted tickets to many of the expensive attractions in their area.

——•——

Instead of going to expensive professional baseball or football game, watch the local kids play in the park. The children will appreciate your support and you'll save money and still get to see all the sporting action that you need.

——•——

Don't waste your hard-earned money seeing new movies. Instead of visiting a theater and paying extortionate prices for food and drink, watch one of the fantastic movies available on commercial TV in the comfort of your own living room. And, if you're worried about missing out on the new movies, don't worry; they'll be on your TV in a couple of years.

——•——

While many Cyclists claim that they like strong showers, they're expensive. An easy way to reduce your personal hygiene costs is to lower the water pressure in your house or apartment.

——•——

While it's important to maintain your garden to keep up your home value, nothing says you have to have a short, green lawn. You can reduce your gardening costs by firing your lawn-mowing person and going for the jungle look. This will attract many wild animals such as snakes, mice, rabbits, etc. By catching them and serving them for dinner, you can also reduce your food costs.

An easy way to cut your power bill is to reduce the brightness of your TV, computer and other devices with screens. While they may be a little bit harder to read, the saving in electricity should more than make up for this inconvenience.

Stay at home. The more time you spend in your home, the longer your shoes will last. And since shoes are expensive, your savings will be considerable.

If you're a water lover and have a large boat or yacht, consider downsizing your large boat and replacing it with a smaller vessel. The savings will be considerable and you'll still get to enjoy the water with your friends and family.

On hot days you can reduce your cooking costs by baking cookies in your car. Instead of using the oven, place your cookie mix on a tray in the back seat of your car. Use a thermometer to monitor the temperature.

If you're one of those people who always wash your hands after you use the toilet, using both sides of the toilet paper will make each roll last twice as long.

Most mechanics recommend changing the oil in your car every 3,000 miles. Cyclists know that by increasing this to 6,000 miles, you'll reduce the amount of oil used by 50 percent.

Never pay for anything you can get for free. Wise Cyclists have adopted this philosophy for years. It's particularly true when it comes to tanning. Instead of taking a trip to your tanning center, visit your local park and stretch out in the sun. While it make take longer in winter to get the tan you desire, it's free.

———•———

The Internet is a great place to find new and innovative ways to save money. When it comes to making your own laundry detergent, there are hundreds of sites that will provide you with a recipe to make your own. When you find a formula that you like, bottle it and sell it to your friends. Encourage them to do the same—and before your know it you'll be sitting on top of your own MLM money making pyramid.

———•———

Instead of taking your family to the mall for an afternoon of window-shopping filled with temptation on a hot summer afternoon, go hiking or biking. The fresh air will be much more refreshing that the recycled air that the mall's air-conditioning system pumps out—and you won't be tempted to spend a cent.

———•———

Instead of calling a plumber to repair a leak in your pipes, use duct tape. This durable material cannot only fix broken pipes, it's also great for rotten floorboards, torn couches and even broken table and desk legs.

When traveling, help yourself to the soap and shampoo that hotels provide for their guests. Leave the blankets and sheets behind—because management will definitely notice if they go missing.

Instead of mailing post cards when you go on vacation, wait till you get home and hand deliver them. An even cheaper method is to email the pics while you're still away.

Instead of buying expensive medications when you're sick, make your own herbal remedies in your kitchen at home.

Don't buy new carpet. Instead, visit your local carpet store after it's closed for the night. Most stores throw away their remnants. Take advantage of this by sewing all of the pieces together to create a unique, multi-colored floor covering that will be the envy of your friends and neighbors.

———·———

Save money on printing by using cheaper fonts such as Garamond on all your documents instead of using Impact or Comic Sans which cost more. You can stretch your ink by an additional 20 to 30 percent by using this method.

———·———

If you live in a building with a gym, take a quick walk down the hall whenever you need to shower or use the bathroom. Think how much money you'll save on electricity, toilet paper, cleaning supplies, soap, etc.

———·———

If the interest rates in your country are low, put your money in an overseas bank that offers higher rates. Many Caribbean countries offer rates of 20 percent or more.

———·———

Instead of eating at expensive restaurants that you like, search the web for coupons. Many restaurants offer discounts to attract new clients. If you're worried about the quality, it's only a minor issue because every restaurant needs to be licensed by your town or county.

———•———

Rip up all the plants in your back garden that are only decorative and replace them with a veggie patch that will cut your food costs. Cyclists who do this get fresh food for a fraction of what your neighbors pay in the supermarket. While it is a little bit of work to cultivate the soil and bottle everything so you can get through the winter, the savings make this a very worthwhile activity.

———•———

Stop wasting money on razor blades or power for your electric razor. Instead, grow a fashionable beard that will keep you warm in winter. As well as saving money, you'll have extra time to get everything on your list done.

———•———

If you're shopping online and fall short of the minimum for free shipping, throw a few extra items in your basket. While you may spend more than you intended, at least you won't waste money on shipping.

———•———

Volunteer to help at your local soup kitchen. While this may seem like a strange way to save money, most institutions

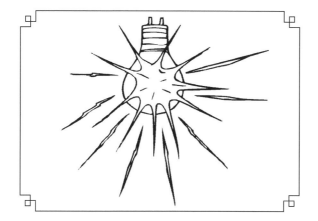

Whenever one of your light bulbs blows, take it to a friend's house and swap it for one that works. Just tell your friend that their bulb blew. Keep good notes—your friends will become suspicious if they need a new bulb every time you visit.

provide their volunteers with a free meal. If there's stuff left over, you can take it home and use it over the next few days.

———•———

Walk around the supermarket parking lot after you've loaded your groceries into your car. Many people don't take the same care that you do, and some even leave valuable items in the cart that you can use at home or return to the store for a refund.

———•———

Instead of wasting money on newspapers to read on the train as you go to work, get in the last carriage of the train. When you get to your destination, walk through all the cars and collect the newspapers and magazines that your fellow commuters have discarded.

———•———

Takeout restaurants are a great place to save money because they allow you to stock up on supplies. Feel free to help yourself to as many napkins, straws, plastic utensils, and ketchup, salt, sugar containers as you need. Work on the principle that if it's not nailed down, it's yours for the taking.

———•———

When traveling, smart Cyclists don't waste their money on bottled water. They simply boil the water they're planning to drink in the coffee maker in their hotel room.

———•———

Bike riding is great for your health. If you live in a good part of town, save money by not purchasing a lock for your bicycle. After all, it's only those people who live in bad areas who need to worry about theft.

———•———

Cyclists know that clothing is overrated. Reduce your laundry bill by wearing fewer items of clothing each day.

— · —

If you're one of those Cyclists who doesn't have a sensitive nose, you can save a fortune when it comes to cleaning your home. Instead of buying commercial cleaning products with pleasant scents, replace them with vinegar and baking powder. This combination will eliminate tough stains and make your home as clean as those expensive commercial products. Just make sure you air out your house before your friends and relatives visit.

— · —

Despite advances in digital technology, some Cyclists still like to read the dead-tree edition of their favorite magazine. Save money by borrowing the issues of the magazine you want from your doctor or dentist's office and return them when you're done. Don't worry if you take a couple of months to get through them—they'll only be marginally more outdated than when you borrowed them.

— · —

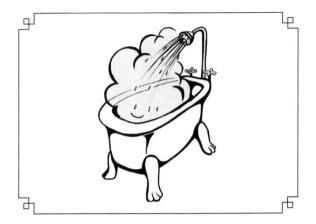

If you live in a house or apartment with more than two people, put a plug in the bathtub when you shower. Everyone else can then take a bath for free.

Instead of getting your hair professionally colored at the salon, pick up a box of color at your local drug store. While the color on the box may not resemble the color in the bottle, you can always redo your color if you're not happy with the result.

Use your home bathroom as little as possible. By waiting until you get to work to do your business, you not only save in toilet paper and soap, you also reduce your water and electricity bills because your employer is picking up the tab. If it takes you a while to do your stuff, you may even qualify for overtime.

———•———

Heating items up in the oven is expensive. To reduce your costs, leave the oven door open after you've finished cooking to heat your apartment.

———•———

If you own a reliable car, cancel your membership to the AAA or your other emergency car service. After all, why should you pay for something that you're unlikely to need.

———•———

If you forget to take your wallet with you when you go out, you'll save a fortune. Most people will happily lend you the money you need for dinner. Since it will take you a few days or a week to pay it back, you can use this time to earn extra interest on your savings. Take care when using this method, because if you leave your license behind, you may end up with a huge fine that will wipe out all your savings.

———•———

Most supermarkets and specialty shops put their bread on sale at the end of the day, and sell it for even less the next day. Since most Cyclists can't tell the difference, it's easy to save money in this area of your food budget.

———•——

Re-use your old sandwich bags. Simply wash them out when you get home, turn them inside out, and hang them out to dry. When you need a new bag to put your lunch in, simply reach for an old bag. While the savings may appear small, every cent you save will add up over time.

———•——

No matter what you do, hair grows. Save money by cutting it yourself. By carefully arranging the mirrors, you shouldn't have too much trouble seeing the back of your head. In a short period of time, you'll easily be able to achieve the perfect cut that you desire.

———•——

Everybody knows how expensive medical services are. Reduce your costs by asking for a discount. Many surgeons, obstetricians, vets, dentists and other specialists will happily cut their prices if you ask. Since they are all professionals, they'll generally give you the same quality services that they give their full-price patients.

———•———

An easy way to reduce the cost of your mobile phone is to charge it at work. Since electricity is expensive, anything you can do to reduce your power bill at home puts more money in your pocket.

———•———

Grow your own food. Instead of planting flowering trees and bushes, plant fruit trees in your garden. In a couple of years when they mature, you'll have an unlimited amount of fruit (depending on how many trees you plant) and you can sell this to your friends and neighbors or barter it for things you really need.

———•———

Don't throw out expensive dress shirts when the collar wears out. Simply remove the collar from the body of the shirt and sew it on backwards. Depending on how often you wear the shirt, you should get several months or years out of it.

———•———

Personal hygiene is expensive if you insist on buying new soap. Instead of wasting your money, visit the auctions

Don't waste money on a paper shredder. Instead, place a few pieces of dog poop in the bags with your bank statements and financial documents. Few thieves will have the nose to go through your stuff.

where motels sell their surplus and invest in partially used bars of soap and very small shampoo containers that still have product in them.

Keep all your lights off at night. Electricity is expensive and lights consume huge amounts of power—especially if you light more than one room at a time. Since walking around in the dark can lead to falls and other injuries, invest in a pair of night vision glasses. This will allow you to wander around at will, without having to worry about costly doctor's bills.

———•———

When it comes to buying gas for your car, never buy from the closest station to your home or office unless it's the cheapest. Simply driving around for a while can uncover stations that are much cheaper than those in your local area.

———•———

Blackout curtains can warm your house in winter and cool it in summer. Unlike during WWII, they're now available in a variety of attractive styles and colors.

———•———

Save money in the laundry room by cutting your dryer sheets in half. Smart Cyclists have discovered that by cutting them in thirds, quarters or fifths they can save even more.

———•———

If you're really serious about saving money, save all your soap slivers. Place them into a shampoo bottle, add a little water and shake. Smart Cyclists have found that soapy water in a bottle makes a great substitute for shampoo or body wash.

———·———

If you're a good driver who rarely has accidents, eliminate your car insurance. All you're doing is subsidizing those bad drivers who don't know how to drive.

———·———

Instead of putting fertilizer on your garden, use coffee grounds. This method is especially effective if you're trying to grow coffee. It also smells a lot better than manure or the fish-based fertilizer products that are so popular today.

———·———

Instead of replacing your disposable contact lenses every couple of weeks like the manufacturer recommends, stretch them to a month or two. Even if you get an occasional eye infection, the costs will probably be less than constantly buying new contact lenses.

———·———

Even though print magazines are almost dead, many manufacturers still give away free cologne samples in specific editions. Use these instead of showering.

———·———

Save dollars on Tupperware and get more value from your Chinese takeout by recycling the plastic and foam takeout containers they use to deliver your food as lunchboxes and food storage containers. Eventually the smell of Chinese food should dissipate.

———

Sell your holiday home. Many Cyclists bought a second home as a status symbol, not realizing how much it costs to run. By downsizing your country palace to a spacious condo, you can reduce your outgoings considerably and still have a nice place to impress the other 99 percent—should they ever see your home.

———

Use cold water to shower. As well as cutting your electricity or gas bill, you'll reduce your water bill since everybody will take shorter showers—especially in winter.

———

Cars are greatly over-rated. Instead of cutting back on your driving, sell your car and use public transport. Even though you may have to get up an hour or two earlier to get to work or visit friends on a Sunday, your bank account will thank you.

———

Eliminating ice cream, cheese and other dairy products will not only reduce your food costs and waist size, it will cut your electricity costs if you use this opportunity to get rid of your refrigerator.

—·—

Replace your house with an RV. Owing a house and a car is expensive. By trading in your house for an RV, smart Cyclists have not only eliminated the need to pay for electricity, taxes, water, etc., they've also been able to get rid of their car. Since most Walmart's offer free overnight parking, you'll never need to pay for accommodation again.

—·—

Cyclists know that one of the best ways to save money is to avoid spending it. Whenever you see something that you want, avoid purchasing it for a month. There's a good chance that the urge to buy the item will have passed by this time and you'll still have the money in your bank account. Just think how much you'll save on food using this method.

—·—

Save money on vacations by planning all your trips in the off-season. While the weather may be less than perfect, and

Instead of buying an address book, use the phone book that the phone company provides free. Simply set aside a couple of hours to cross out the names of all the people that you don't know.

your children may be forced to miss school, the short-term savings should more than make up for the inconvenience.

———•———

To reduce your car expenses, don't let your children drive your car until they're over 25. Not only will you reduce your risk of them having an accident, you'll cut your insurance rates by 50 percent or more.

———•———

Soda is expensive and bad for you. By eliminating this unnecessary beverage from your diet, you can save a huge amount of money. Think about the cost. If you drink four cans per day and pay $1.50 per can, you will save almost $200 per month. If you drink more, the savings will be even greater.

————

If you're feeling lonely and want to save some cash, move in with your kids. After all, you brought your kids into the world, raised them, and paid for their food, toys and education. To say the least, they owe you. This arrangement will not only save you a fortune, it will make your life easier if you use your grandchildren to run errands and pick up all the things you need. When they're old enough, you'll even have a free driver who will pay for the gas and all the repairs on their car.

————

First class travel is very expensive. By downgrading to business class, you can save a fortune. To tell the truth, those flatbed seats are really overrated.

————

Drive carefully and obey all the traffic laws. Tickets cost Cyclists money, run the risk of jail time and force up your insurance rates.

—·—

If you've written a book, ask your friends and family to look at it and give you their comments before you publish it. You'll not only get their expertise and insights FREE—you'll also get all the opinions you need to make it a best seller. Thanks everybody.

—·—

Afterword

Raising a family is tougher today than it's ever been. In the past, many people made a few extra dollars by sending their wife out to work for a few hours each week to earn a little extra cash. This is no longer an option, because most spouses are already working fulltime.

Other families survived by allowing their school-aged children to work. Teenage unemployment, school restrictions and crime make this difficult—if not impossible—in many areas.

This has caused people to look for new ways to make and save money. As a result, an entire industry has developed and hundreds of people earn their income writing tips for newspapers, blogs and magazines. Others write books.

While there's nothing wrong with this, many of the tips these people come up with are so silly, they're unbelievable. Rather than fight this trend, I've decided to embrace it. Every tip in this book has appeared in at least one article or blog. That's right, even the silly ones that make no sense.

As a result, it's important to use your judgment and take care implementing the valuable information contained in this book. Think about how long each tip will take to implement, how much your time is worth and if the short-term savings outweigh the long-term costs. Disregarding the car manufacturer's advice on when to change your oil may reduce the amount of money you spend on oil, but could result in costly repairs.

Likewise, reusing tissues, dental floss or other personal hygiene products could result in major medical bills or have other long-term health implications. And, to put it simply, just because something is in writing, doesn't mean it's true, a good idea or even useful.

In case you're wondering, none of the tips in this book have been vetted by my crack legal team to ensure that they're legal, ethical or even moral. The reason is because many of them are not.

And, while every tip in this book is guaranteed to reduce the amount of money you outlay at some point in your life, they will change the way people perceive you. If you implement them all, everybody will think you're a cheap, money-grabbing bastard who will do anything to save a buck and avoid your obligations. And, again, to put it simply, they'd be right.

That said, have a great life and feel free to use this book for the purpose for which it was intended.

Mark Geoffrey Young
New York, NY.
www.dolyttle.com

ACKNOWLEDGEMENTS

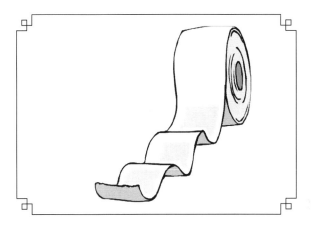

Reduce the amount of toilet paper you waste by buying two-ply toilet paper and splitting it in two. This simple money saving method gives you two rolls of toilet paper for the price of one.

Writing books is hard. Not, for the writer, but for everybody else who has to put up with the strange hours, erratic behavior, nutty demands and general grumpiness.

For putting up with me, I say thanks to my son Jackson and my wife Pam. To my clients, I say thanks for your input. Many of you provided me with some of the best tips in this book.

And to the person who wrote the introduction, thanks for nothing. Nobody seemed to get the concept of this book, and as a result, nobody was willing to write the forward for free and I had to do it myself. I guess that's what happens when you decide to write a book.

Thankyou to everybody who helped out and saved me money including: Eastchester Library, Greenburgh Library, Scarsdale Library, Hazel Bradley, Jenny Berich, Roger Cawkwell, Darlene Duran, Cari Dyslin, Robert Johnstone, Nora Phykitt, Greg Rapport, Pam Schancupp, Diane Young, Mike Young, Robert Young, Tina Yun, John Yun, and all the other people who contributed their tips to this book. Thanks again.

.

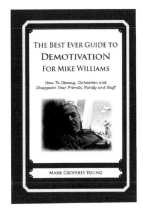
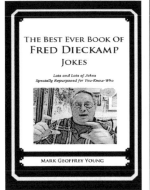
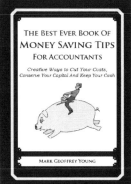

If you'd like to make this book your own, why not order a personalized copy for yourself or a friend. Simply go to www.dolyttle.com and order a copy of The Best Ever Book of YOUR NAME Jokes, The Best Ever Guide to Demotivation for YOUR NAME, or The Best Ever Book of Money Saving Tips for YOUR NAME.

We'll put your name and picture on the cover and throughout the book. Or, if you'd rather, simply order one of the many titles available.

At $19.95 per copy it's a great deal. Simply go to www.dolyttle.com.

ORDER! FORM

Dolyttle & Seamore
198 Garth Road Suite 2DD
Scarsdale, NY 10583
212-496-8771 • info@dolyttle.com
(For faster service go to www.dolyttle.com)

Name		
Address		Apt.
City	State	ZIP
Country		
Email		
Phone		

Title:
The Best Ever Book of _____Jokes
The Best Ever Guide to Demotivation for _____

If you don't have a friend, don't worry about it. We'll nominate somebody be your friend, at absolutely no additional cost. Each book is $19.95 plus $3.99 shipping for the first book and $2.00 for each additional copy. Call for pricing for large orders and corporate prices.

WWW.DOLYTTLE.COM

On the next couple of pages, you'll see a selection of our current titles. Order either the demotivation book, the joke book or both.

OCCUPATIONS

Account Executive, Acccountant, Actor, Acupuncturist, Administrative Assistant, Administrator, Aide, Air Force, Air Traffic Controller, Ambulance Officer, Analyst, Anesthesiologist, Announcer, Antique Dealer, Architect, Army, Assistant, Astronomer, Athlete, Audiologist, Auditor, Author, Baker, Balloon Artist, Banker, Barber, Barista, Bartender, Beautician, Beekeeper, Benefit Manager, Bill Collector, Biologist, Bodybuilder, Book Seller, Bookkeeper, Bricklayer, Builder, Building Manager, Bus Driver, Business Owner, Butcher, Camera Operator, Camp Counselor, Camp Director, Candy Store Owner, Car Salesman, Caregiver, Carpenter, Carpet Layer, Carpet Salesperson, Cartographer, Chauffeur, Chef, Chemical Engineer, Chemist, Chiropractor, Cinematographer, Civil Engineer, Civil Servant, Claims Adjuster, Clerk, Clown, Coach, Coast Guard, Company Director, Compliance Officer, Computer Engineer, Computer Operator, Computer, Programmer, Conductor, Conference Producer, Congressman, Conservationist, Cook, Copy Editor Corrections Officer, Counselor, Courier Criminal, Cyclist, Dancer Data Entry Operator, Debt Collector, Deli Owner, Delivery Person, Dental Assistant, Dental Hygienist, Dental Technician, Dentist, Dermatologist, Designer, Detailer, Detective, Dispatcher, Doctor, Dog Walker, Doorman, Dressmaker, Driver, Drug Dealer, Dry Cleaner, Electrician, Engineer, Engraver, Entertainer, Entrepreneur, Environmental Engineer, Epidemiologist, Episcopalian, Executive, Exporter, Falcons' Fan, Farmer, Fire Fighter, Fireman, Fisherman, Fitness Instructor, Flight Attendant, Flight Engineer, Florist, Flower Seller, Food Technologist, Funeral Director, Furniture Maker, Furniture Salesperson, Garbage Collector, Gardener, Geologist, Golfer, Graphic Designer, Grave Digger, Grocer, Guard, Hairdresser, Handyman, Hardware Store, Owner, Historian, Horticulturist, Host, Hostess, Human Resource, Consultant, Human Resource, Manager, Importer, Industrial Engineer, Information Systems, Manager, Information Technology, Manager, Inspector, Instructor, Intelligence Officer, Interpreter, Janitor, Jeweler, Journalist, Judge, Laborer, Labourer, Landscaper, Law Clerk, Lawyer, Life Guard, Locksmith, Machinist, Magician, Mail Carrier, Mail Sorter, Mailman, Makeup Artist, Manager, Managing Director, Manicurist, Marines, Marriage Counselor, Mathematician, Mechanic, Medical Assistant, Medical Technician, Messenger, Meteorologist, Meter Reader, Midwife, Miner, Minister, Model, Musician, National Guard, Naturalist, Naturopath, Navy, Notary Public, Nuclear Engineer, Nuclear Physicist, Nurse, Nursing Aide, Obstetrician, Occupational Therapist, Optician, Orthodontist, Paralegal, Parking Inspector, Parole Officer, Party Planner, Payroll Clerk, Pediatric Oncologist, Pediatrician, Pharmacist, Pharmacy, Technician, Philosopher, Physical Therapist, Physician, Physician's Assistant, Physician's Assistant, Physicist, Physiotherapist, Pilot, Plumber, Podiatrist, Police, Political Scientist, Postal Carrier, Postal Worker, Postman, Postmaster, Potter, PR Executive, President, Priest, Printer, Prison Guard, Prison Officer, Probation Officer, Producer, Professor, Programmer, Projectionist, Proofreader, Prostitute, Psychiatric Nurse, Psychiatrist, Psychic, Psychologist, Public Servant, Purchasing Manager, Rabbi, Radiographer, Radiologist, Real Estate, Refrigeration Mechanic, Registrar, Repairman, Reporter, Roofer, Rubbish Collector, Sailor, Sales Manager Joke, Salesman, Salesperson, Scientist, Secretary, Security Guard Joke, Senator, Sheriff, Shoemaker, Shop Assistant, Sign Writer, Singer, Skin Care Specialist, Small Business Owner, Social Worker, Socialist, Sociologist, Sound Technician, Speech Therapist, Spy, Statistician, Student, Subeditor, Superintendent, Surfer, Surgeon, Surveillance Officer, Surveyor, Swimmer, Swimming Instructor, Tailor, Taxi Driver, Teacher, Teaching Assistant, Technician, Technologist, Technology Writer, Telemarketer, Therapist, Ticket Collector, Tire Dealer, Tire Technician, Title Examiner, Tour Guide, Trainer, Travel Agent, Truck Driver, Tutor, Tyre Dealer, Tyre Technician, Umpire, Undertaker, Underwriter, Upholsterer, Urban Planner, Urologist, Usher, Veterinarian, Waiter, Waitress, Web Designer, Welder, Window Washer, Zookeeper, Zoologist

NATIONALITIES

Afghan, Albanian, Algerian, American, Andorran, Angolan, Anguillan, Antiguan, Argentinean, Armenian, Australian, Austrian, Azerbaijani, Bahamian, Bahraini, Bangladeshi, Barbadian, Batswana, Belarusian, Belgian, Belizean, Beninese, Bermudian, Bhutanese, Bolivian, Bosnian, Brazillian, British, Bruneian, Bulgarian, Burkinabe, Burmese, Burundian, Cambodian, Cameroonian, Canadian, Cape Verdian, Caymanian, Central African, Chadian, Chilean, Chinese, Christmas Islander, Cocos Islander, Colombian, Comoran, Congolese, Costa Rican, Croat, Cuban, Cypriot, Czech, Danish, Djibouti, Dominica, Dutch, East Timorese, Ecuadorean, Egyptian, Emirati, English, Equatoguinean, Eritrean, Estonian, Ethiopian, Falkland Islander, Fijian, Filipino, Finnish, French, Gabonese, Gambian, Georgian, German, Ghanaian, Gibraltarian, Greek, Greenlander, Grenadian, Guadeloupian, Guatemalan, Guianese, Guinea-Bissauan, Guinean, Guyanese, Haitian, Herzegovinian, Honduran, Hungarian, Icelandic, Indian, Indonesian, Iraqi, Irish, Israeli, Italian, Jamaican, Japanese, Jordanian, Kazakhstani, Kenyan, Kiribati, Kittian, Korean, Kuwaiti, Kyrgyzstani, Laotian, Latvian, Lebanese, Liberian, Libyan, Liechtensteiner, Lithuanian, Luxembourger, Macedonian, Madagascan, Mahorais, Malagasy, Malawian, Malaysian, Maldivian, Malian, Maltese, Marshallese, Martinican, Mauritanian, Mauritian, Mexican, Micronesian, Moldovan, Monacan, Mongolian, Montenegrin, Montserratian, Moroccan, Mozambican, Myanmarese, Namibian, Nauruan, Nepalese, Netherlander, Nevisian, New Zealand, New Zealander, Nicaraguan, Niger, Nigerian, Nigerien, Norwegian, Omani, Pakistani, Palauan, Palestinian, Panamanian, Papua, New Guinean, Paraguayan, Peruvian, Polish, Portuguese, Puerto Rican, Qatari, Reunionese, Romanian, Russian, Rwandan, Saint Helenian, Saint Lucian, Saint Vincentian, Salvadoran, Sammarinese, Sao Tomean, Saudi Arabian, Scottish, Senegalese, Serbian, Seychellois, Sierra Leonean, Singaporean, Slovakian, Slovene, Solomon Islander, Somali, Somalian, South African, Spaniard, Spanish, Sri Lankan, Sudan, Sudanese, Surinamer, Swazi, Swedish, Swiss, Syrian, Taiwanese, Tajik, Tanzanian, Thai, Tobagonian, Togolese, Tongan, Trinidadian, Tunisian, Turkish, Turkmen, Tuvaluan, Ugandan, Ukrainian, Uruguayan, Uzbekistani, Vanuatu, Venezuelan, Vietnamese, Virgin Islander, Welsh, Yemeni, Zambian, Zimbabwean and others

SPORTS

Adventure, Archery, Badminton, Athlete, Baseball, Basketball, Bodybuilder, Bowling, Boxing, Canoeist, Coach, Cricket, Cyclist, Dancer, Diving, Fencing, Fisherman, Fitness Instructor Football, Golfer, Gymnast, Handball, Hiking, Hockey, Horse Riding, Hunting, Jockey, Kayaker, Mountaineer, Orienteering, Pilot, Ping Pong, Polo, Racing, Racquetball, Referee, Rower, Rugby, Runner, Sailor, Skier, Shooter, Soccer Softball, Squash, Surfer, Swimmer, Swimming Instructor, Table Tennis, Trainer, Tramping, Umpire, Volleyball, Weightlifter, Wrestling

Baseball

Angels, Astros, Athletics, Blue Jays, Braves, Brewers, Cardinals, Cubs, Diamondbacks, Dodgers, Giants, Indians, Mariners, Marlins, Mets, Nationals, Orioles, Padres, Phillies, Pirates, Rangers, Rays, Red Sox, Reds, Rockies, Royals, Tigers, Twins, White Sox, Yankees

Baseball

76ers, Blazers, Bobcats, Bucks, Bulls, Cavaliers, Celtics, Clippers, Grizzlies, Hawks, Heat, Hornets, Jazz, Kings, Knicks, Lakers, Magic, Mavericks, Nets, Nuggets, Pacers, Pistons, Raptors, Rockets, Spurs, Suns, Thunder, Timberwolves, Warriors, Wizards

American Football
Football, Soccer, 49ers, Bears, Bengals, Bills, Broncos, Browns, Buccaneers, Cardinals, Chargers, Chiefs, Colts, Cowboys, Dolphins, Eagles, Falcons, Giants, Jaguars, Jets, Lions, Packers, Panthers, Patriots, Raiders, Rams, Ravens, Redskins, Saints, Seahawks, Steelers, Texans, Titans, Vikings

English Football / English Soccer
Football, Soccer, Arsenal, Aston Villa, Chelsea, Everton, Fulham, Liverpool, Manchester City, Manchester United, Newcastle United, Norwich City, Queens Park, Rangers, Reading, Southampton, Stoke City, Sunderland, Swansea City, Tottenham Hotspur, West Bromwich, Albion, West Ham United, Wigan Athletic

SEXUAL
Gay, Homosexual, Lesbian, Masturbator, Nudist, Pervert, Prostitute, Transsexual, Wanker

MEDICAL
Acupuncturist, Ambulance Officer, Anesthesiologist Biologist, Chemist, Chiropractor, Counselor, Dental Assistant, Dental Hygienist, Dental Technician, Dermatologist, Doctor, Naturopath, Nurse, Nursing Aide, Obstetrician, Occupational Therapist, Optician, Orthodontist, Pediatric Oncologist, Pediatrician, Pharmacist, Pharmacy, Technician, Physician, Physician's Assistant Joke, Physical Therapist, Podiatrist, Physiotherapist, Psychiatric Nurse, Psychologist, Psychiatrist, Radiologist, Radiographer, Surgeon, Therapist, Undertaker, Urologist, Veterinarian

GENERAL
Blind, Blond, Boy Scout, Brunette, Cat Lover, Conservationist, Criminal, Dog Lover, Drug Dealer, Essex Girl, Girl Scout, Pilot, Redhead, Redneck, Vegan, Vegetarian

CREATIVE
Actor, Artist, Author, Balloon Artist, Cinematographer, Clown, Conductor, Dancer, Designer, Dressmaker, Entertainer, Graphic Designer, Hat Maker, Pilot, Singer, Woodworker, Writer

RELIGION
Atheist, Baptist, Born Again, Buddhist, Catholic, Christian, Episcopalian, Jehovah's Witness, Jewish, Mormon, Muslim, Pagan, Protestant, Scientologist, Witch, Unitarian

POLITICAL
Barack Obama, Christian Democrat, Communist, Congressman, Conservative, Criminal, Democrat, Glenn Beck, Independent, Labour, Liberal, Libertarian, Michael Bloomberg, Michele Bachmann, Mitt Romney, Newt Gingrich, Non-Voter, Republican, Senator, Social Democrat, Socialist, Tea Party

Printed in Great Britain
by Amazon.co.uk, Ltd.,
Marston Gate.